An Integrated Pathway For Assessment And Support

For children with complex needs and their families

A Manual For Service Development

030014

An Integrated Pathway
for Assessment and Support

Published in 2003 by Interconnections
9 Pitt Avenue
Worcester
WR4 0PL
Tel/Fax: 01905 23255

Printed in the UK by Interconnections

ISBN 0-9540976-1-0

Dedicated to the memory of

Nicholas Limbrick

About the author

Peter Limbrick has a background in special education and he established the registered charity *One Hundred Hours* which worked in the 1990s to develop and validate a keyworker-based support system for families who have a baby or young child with disabilities and complex needs. He now chairs *The Handsel Trust* which grew out of One Hundred Hours as a campaign for effective support for these families in the UK. Peter is an independent consultant to statutory and voluntary/independent services in the UK and Ireland.

Acknowledgements

The impetus for this manual began while I was working with families in the One Hundred Hours project. It was then that I realised the high levels of unmet need experienced by families who have babies and young children with complex needs. Since then I have worked with very many parents, practitioners, service managers and teams within health, education, social services and the voluntary/independent sector who want to provide better support for families and who are striving to join services together into an integrated approach. This manual is based on all the good practice I have encountered in this work and on my discussions with very many people about how to remedy fragmentation in service provision. My sincere thanks go to all of these people. I wish also to thank Pat McKelvey, Manager of Services for Children with Complex Needs in Halton Primary Care Trust, and Gudrun Limbrick-Spencer of The Handsel Trust for their helpful comments.

Contents

Introduction

This manual is about babies and young children with disabilities who have complex needs. They represent an expanding population and they highlight the need for services to be more organised, more integrated, more family-centred and more accountable. The manual suggests how health, education, social services and the voluntary/independent sector can work together to provide these children and their families with an effective service.

Some terms used in this manual

Children with complex needs. Some services define these children as children who need continuing support from two or more practitioners from one or more agencies. Another approach is to define them as children (and families) who require a complicated service. This group will include some children with continuing health needs and some with life-limiting conditions.

Agencies, services and localities. 'Agency' refers to the statutory agencies of health, education and social services and to voluntary and independent organisations. Within these agencies there is a variety of services, teams, centres, projects and units which help young children with complex needs. This manual uses the term 'service' to represent them all and assumes that most services will have some integration between disciplines if not between agencies. The term 'locality' is used for the administrative/geographical area covered by the service or agency.

Practitioner. This word is used to refer to all the professionals or paid workers who help the child and family. It can include (in alphabetical order) dieticians, geneticists, health visitors, keyworkers, nurses, nursery nurses, paediatricians, play leaders, Portage teachers, psychologists, social workers, specialist teachers, therapists and others. Practitioners who have a hands-on involvement with the child and family are distinguished from 'service managers' though it is recognised that in many cases it is a dual role.

Support. 'Support' is used in this manual to bring together many elements of service provision. Support for the child includes provision of play activity, education, therapy, treatment and care. Support for the parents can include emotional support, provision of information, mentoring and advocacy. Support for the family can also include support for siblings, grandparents and other significant members of the family - however it chooses to define itself.

Assessment events and assessment processes. There are many approaches to assessment. At one end of the spectrum is the one-day child-assessment *event* and at the other is the family-centred assessment *process* over a much longer period of time. Assessment and support are not mutually exclusive. The practitioner is learning more about the child and family while he or she is providing support and, ideally, offering relevant support during any assessment activity. This is reflected here in the term 'assessment/support process'

The purpose of this manual

This manual is intended as an aid to service development for all services and agencies which support babies and pre-school children with complex needs and their families. It encourages and facilitates the description of a service in terms of a pathway which can be represented diagrammatically and acknowledges that pathways will be unique to their own locality. The manual can be used by services at increasing levels of integration. It can be used by a multi-disciplinary team to describe and then improve its own integrated service. It can be used by a panel of senior managers from two or more agencies to create an integrated multi-agency pathway for the locality.

The manual does not offer any new invention or theory. It brings together models of good practice which the author has seen in all parts of the UK and Ireland and builds them into an accountable system which can be described, resourced, monitored and evaluated. The approach embodies the spirit of the NHS Plan by advocating modernisation, some breaking down of professional boundaries and improved partnership between agencies.

The layout of the manual

Integrated pathways discusses the merits of integrated pathways and offers a structure for describing and enhancing a pathway for a multi-disciplinary or multi-agency service.

A flexible approach to assessment discusses assessment procedures and suggests a flexible approach which can reduce waiting times.

Designing an integrated pathway offers a detailed approach to designing an integrated pathway which incorporates the Team-around-the-Child model.

In conclusion suggests some key issues to consider in modernising services and offers sources for further information.

Integrated pathways

What is an integrated pathway?

For a child with complex needs, who might need specialist care and nursing support and specialist help to develop motor, perception, communication, social and cognitive skills, and for the family, who might need counselling, financial advice and help with equipment and housing, there can be many practitioners, services and agencies which might operate more or less separately from each other. Each service can have its own referral system, waiting list, assessment procedure and working method and each can have different terminology, criteria and rules. The result is the service maze which mystifies parents, practitioners and service managers alike. The current appeals for co-ordinated and integrated services recognise the damage such fragmentation can cause to families. Parents waste time, energy and money trying to get the best service possible. The consequence very often is increased stress for the family and reduced learning opportunities for the child.

Part of the solution is to map the connections between practitioners, services and agencies in the locality. The process of producing the map will be the beginning of an attempt to reduce the confusion and complexity. Such a map will have within it many different pathways for children with particular needs. Each pathway will describe the journey the child and family make through the major phases of referral, assessment, support and review.

Children with complex needs require an integrated pathway which reflects collaboration between agencies, services and practitioners and which describes a coherent, seamless and responsive service for the child and family. Though the initiative works towards the ideal of a single all-embracing multi-agency pathway, we must acknowledge that this is a process which might take many years and then might have to remain incomplete. This is a factor of the multiplicity of need of some children and the pervasive impact on all aspects of family functioning in the first years.

There are clear advantages in creating a diagram of a service's integrated pathway for children with complex needs, whether it is contained within one service or spans two or more agencies:

1. This will be a collaborative process involving a number of practitioners and their discussions will inevitably lead to improved understanding and integration between them.
2. The process will locate the pathway within the bigger service map and this will expose duplications and gaps in provision.
3. The process will suggest possibilities for inviting additional practitioners, services and agencies into the pathway and will provide a basis for discussions with them.
4. The process will indicate where families experience waiting times and might indicate solutions.
5. The process might indicate opportunities for offering earlier support.
6. The process will indicate where additional resources are required.
7. Once a service is described in this way it can be properly documented, monitored and evaluated.
8. Parents will have a clear picture of what is offered, they will know where they are at the moment and what to expect next.
9. Practitioners will know what the integrated service is, how they fit into it and where they are at any one time with a particular family.
10. The process provides an excellent opportunity to look objectively and critically at the service as a whole. The time invested in this will bring great benefits to families and to practitioners.

Designing an integrated pathway

Some services will already have a diagram to accurately represent the service they offer to children with complex needs and their families. Some services will have an incomplete diagram which does not reflect all the collaborations between practitioners, services and agencies and some will have no diagram at all. The remainder of this section is a guide to creating a comprehensive diagram for an integrated service and recognises five major phases:

1. Meeting the new child and family - The Meeting Phase.
2. Learning about the child and family - The Learning Phase.
3. Planning how to support the child and family - The Planning Phase.
4. Supporting the child and family - The Support Phase.
5. Reviewing the support for the child and family - The Review Phase.

A diagram representing an outline pathway appears overpage.

A pathway diagram in outline

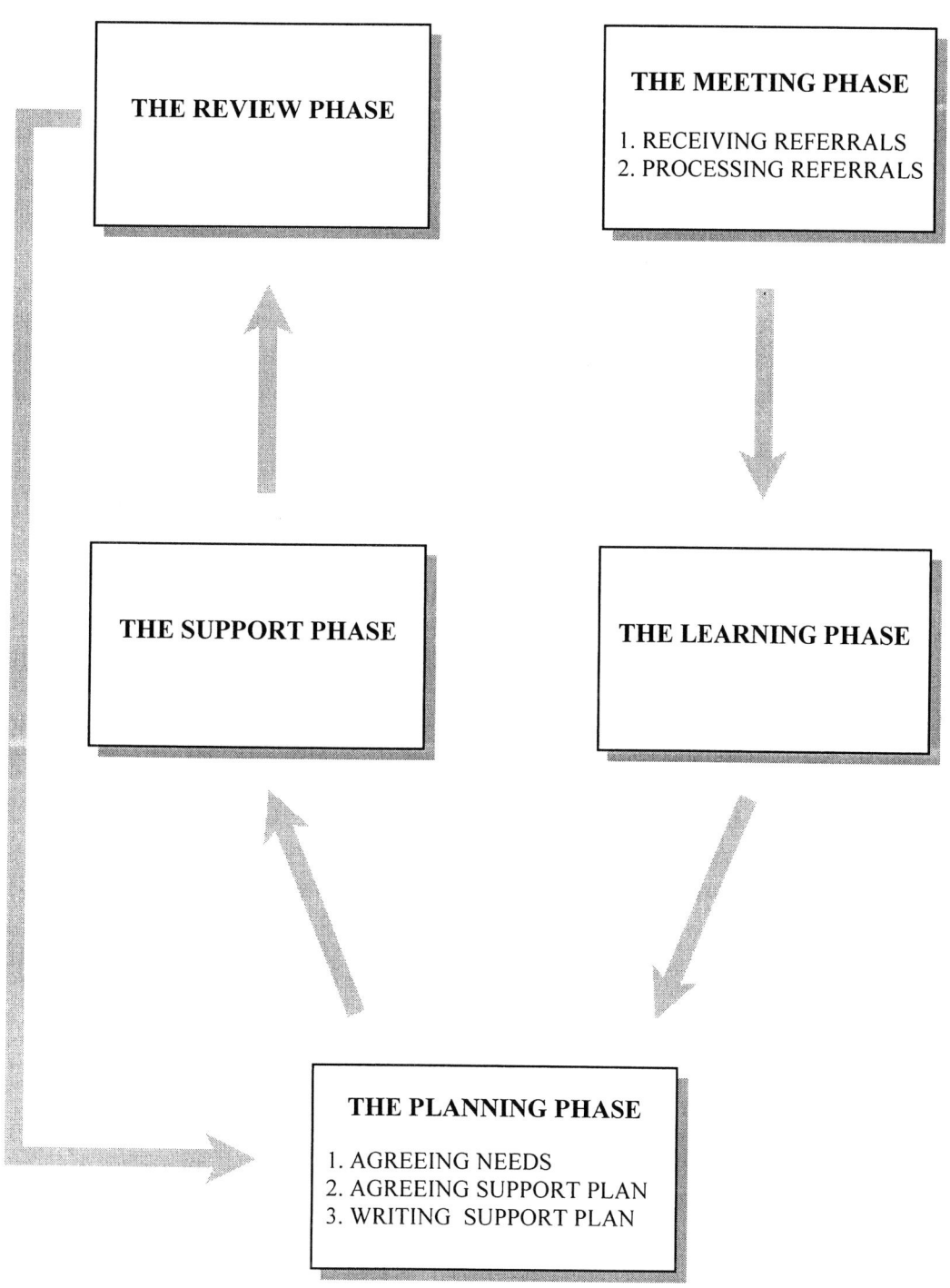

An Integrated Pathway for Assessment and Support

Topics to consider in describing and enhancing an integrated pathway

Whether the objective is to agree a diagrammatic representation of the journey the child and family make within the service or to go further and enhance integration, the task will be a collaboration between a number of practitioners. Deciding who should be involved is the first part of the process and the first opportunity for increasing integration. In some cases it will be the multi-disciplinary team and in other cases it will be practitioners and senior managers from two or more agencies. If the task is to create a more effective service, two or more parents should be invited as representatives of local parents to contribute to the discussions (parents can be disadvantaged when on their own in meetings). The discussions should be informed by local, national and international recommendations and requirements. At the time of writing national documents include *Together from the Start, Framework for the Assessment of Children in Need and their Families, Special Educational Needs Code of Practice* and the emerging *National Service Framework for Children.* Topics to consider in describing and enhancing the pathway include -

* process
* flexibility
* parents
* administration
* waiting
* integration
* performance

The following section explains each of these topics and poses some relevant questions to aid discussion at *each phase* of the pathway. The questions are offered as a guide for discussion only. Creating an integrated pathway might be a process lasting months and years. Considering all the above discussion topics for every phase all in one go might be too demanding of time. Also, addressing a particular requirement in the pathway as a whole does not always mean it has to be addressed in each separate phase. For example, it would not be appropriate to hold a meeting with parents at each part of each phase although it is relevant to keep in mind at all times the question of how parents are involved. The integrated pathway must represent the best possible service within existing resources and not an unattainable ideal.

Process. This is the agreed description of what happens during the meeting phase, learning phase, etc. Questions for each phase include:

Who manages or co-ordinates the process in each phase?
Is the process documented?

Flexibility. By definition, a service which is needs-led must contain within it opportunities for flexibility. No service can offer total flexibility. Discussion between managers, practitioners and parents can categorise tasks and working methods into those which, for whatever reason, cannot be altered or omitted, those which can be altered in compelling circumstances and those which are easily adapted to each family's particular needs. Once this distinction is made, parents and practitioners will be clear about the potential for, and limits to, flexibility. Questions for each phase include:

Within each phase where are the opportunities for responding flexibly to individual children and families?
Can the service change its approach as the abilities and needs of the child and family change?

Parents. Parents must be given good information about the service and must be fully involved in planning and reviewing the service for their child and family. Services must empower parents by giving up some of the control they have exercised in the past. However, power should not lie totally with either professionals or parents. The ideal is a balance which recognises parents' caring, commitment and expertise and the training, experience and expertise of practitioners. This balance will be achieved by negotiation at the level of service design and at the level of planning the service to each individual family. Questions for each phase include:

How are parents informed?
How are parents involved?
How are parents empowered?
Can some sessions be timed to involve a working parent?

Administration. Some services will benefit by identifying a larger administrative role in some phases of the integrated pathway. For practitioners who are spending additional time in collaborating with other practitioners or in chairing multi-disciplinary meetings, clerical support will be a great asset. This can save practitioners' time in arranging meetings, typing minutes and mailing them out. The administration department attached to a service or agency could also be involved in driving the various procedures on the pathway. An example might be arranging a particular meeting to conform to the time limits built into the pathway. This would require knowing who needs to be at the meeting and what their availability is. Administrative staff can also be involved in collecting data for use in strategic planning. Questions for each phase include:

Is there administrative support?
Is clerical help available?
Can this phase be driven by administration?
How is this phase resourced?

Waiting. Waiting times and waiting lists are directly related to resource levels but there is often some room for manoeuvre when the procedures are examined objectively and creatively. For example, it might be possible to offer anxious parents some support while waiting for assessment and it might be possible to embark on some support for the child while waiting for a diagnosis. Questions for each phase include:

Is there a waiting list at this phase of the pathway?
What causes this waiting list?

Integration. At each phase of the pathway the discussion can focus on opportunities for involving other practitioners, services and agencies. Questions for each phase include:

What are the opportunities for inviting other practitioners, services and agencies to integrate their work into this part of the pathway?

Performance. The effectiveness of the service at each phase of the pathway should be monitored and evaluated. The discussion can consider what information to collect, what standards to use to measure performance and how to report the findings. Questions for each phase include:

What standards can be applied to each phase?
What factors demonstrate effectiveness?
How can parents report their experience of each phase to the service?
Who monitors and evaluates each phase?
Who sees the evaluation?

The following section suggests discussion questions which are relevant to each particular phase.

The Meeting Phase

This first phase includes receiving referrals and processing them as a prelude to the assessment/support process.

1. Receiving referrals

Process
Has the service reached a clear agreement on the criteria for referral?
Does the service disseminate good information to people who refer about what the service does, about referral criteria and about how to refer?
Do all referrals come through a single point of entry?
Who is responsible for receiving them?
What does this person do with each referral?

Parents
Are parents told a referral has been received?
Are they given information about the service and the integrated pathway?
Does a practitioner arrange to meet the family at this stage?
Can parents refer their own child?
If so, how do they learn about the service?
Who first meets self-referring parents?

Waiting
The time a family has to wait to be referred to the service is not the responsibility of the service. But is it possible to collect data from families about these waiting times in the interests of enhancing early intervention in the locality?

Integration
What are the opportunities for inviting other practitioners, services or agencies to share in agreeing criteria, sending information out and sharing the single point of entry?

2. The intake process

Process
Is this performed by a single practitioner or a panel?
How is it decided whether or not to accept the child into the service?
Are the agreed criteria the same as the referral criteria?

What provision is made for children who are not accepted?
- Is the person who referred informed?
- Are the parents informed?
What other decisions are made at the intake process?
Does it plan the learning phase?
Are particular practitioners assigned to the family at this stage?
Is a keyworker/care manager assigned to the family?
Are other practitioners, services or agencies informed that this child has now entered the service?

Flexibility

Can a decision be made at this stage to offer a particular family some immediate support on a 'first-aid' basis?

Parents

Does a practitioner do a home visit?
Is this before or after the intake process?
Are parents invited to the intake meeting?
How are parents told the outcome of the intake process?
Are they told in writing?

Administration

Are notes kept of the intake process for each child?
Are dates set for events during later parts of the pathway?
Is the child entered on a multi-agency database?
Is data collected about referrals for use in strategic planning?

Waiting

How often do intake meetings happen?
What is the maximum time a family might have to wait?

Performance

What is the period of time between referral and completion of the process?

The Learning Phase

Though something will be already known about the child and family there will need to be a period of learning more about their needs before a full support system can be put in place.

Process

Who designs the learning phase for each child?

Who co-ordinates the learning phase for each child?

Are particular practitioners assigned to the family at this stage?

Is a keyworker/care manager assigned to the family?

How are the findings of the learning phase recorded?

Which practitioners, services or agencies are informed of the findings?

Flexibility

Is there a fixed assessment procedure for all children or is there more than one possible approach?

If the latter, what criteria apply in deciding the approach to be used?

Can the child be observed at home and in any placement he or she attends?

Are other practitioners, services or agencies who know the child invited to provide information?

Parents

Are parents given written information in advance about the learning phase?

Can they help design the learning phase for their child and family?

Are they invited to provide information about their child's abilities and needs in as much detail as they wish?

Are their questions incorporated into the assessment procedure?

Can the learning phase focus on any particular challenges they are facing at that time (e.g. family stress, sleep, behaviour, nutrition)?

Who supports the family during the learning phase?

Can the child and/or family be offered any necessary 'first-aid' support during the learning phase or while on the waiting list for the assessment procedure?

Are parents given a written account of the findings?

Administration

Can time limits be set for events within the learning phase?

Is there help for arranging meetings, writing reports and mailing them out?

Integration

What are the opportunities for inviting other practitioners, services or agencies to contribute to the collection of information and to the document which records the findings of the learning phase?

Is there a standardised multi-disciplinary or multi-agency form for

recording the findings of the learning phase?
If so, who receives it when it is completed?

Performance
What is the period of time between referral and the start of the learning phase?
What is the period of time between referral and the end of the learning phase?

The Planning Phase

This phase has two stages within it:

1. **Agreeing the needs of the child and family.** This is an essential phase following the collection of a body of relevant information about the child and family and preceding the writing of the support plan. Parents and practitioners are involved in the process with due weight given to the parental view. The needs of the child and family can be divided into three categories: those for which the service can offer support, those which require a referral to another service or agency and those for which there is no available support at this time.
2. **Planning how to support the child and family.** Support for the child can include care, nursing, therapy and education. For parents and other family members it can include counselling, benefits advice, mentoring, advocacy, and support to become co-workers. For siblings it can be a wide range of interventions. The planning process results in a written family support plan which describes in some detail the support to be offered by the agencies, services and practitioners involved in the pathway.

Though it is necessary to recognise that the planning process must be preceded by an agreement about needs, the two processes are dealt with together here.

Process
Who co-ordinates the planning phase for each individual child?
What is the process for agreeing the needs of the child and family?
What is the process for agreeing what support the service can offer the child and family?
Is the agreed plan written down in some way?
Who gets copies of it?

Parents

Does the discussion about needs happen with parents present?
Does the discussion to plan support happen with parents present?
If not how are they involved?
Are parents given a written family support plan?

Administration

Can time limits be set for events within the planning phase?
Is there help for arranging meetings, writing reports and mailing them out?

Integration

What are the opportunities for increasing the number of practitioners, services or agencies who contribute to the family support plan?

Performance

What is the period of time between referral and giving the parents the finished support plan?

The Support Phase

This phase is the one that gives meaning to the whole pathway. This is where the work happens to help the child develop, to support the parents in their efforts to adapt and to help the family survive the first months and years. This is worth emphasising here because there are some localities where a carefully planned assessment procedure results in very little support.

Process

Who co-ordinates support for each individual child?
Are particular practitioners assigned to the family at this stage?
Is a keyworker/care manager assigned to the family?
Are the practitioners who provide support the same ones who were involved in the assessment procedure?
If not, what is the communication process?
What records are kept during the support process?
Who holds the records?
Who sees them?

Flexibility

Is there flexibility in the balance between sessions at home and sessions at the centre/clinic?

Can frequency, timing and duration of sessions vary according to need?

Can practitioners link with statutory/voluntary/independent placements the child attends to share observations, goals and skills?

Parents

Are parents invited to be co-workers on the child's programmes?

If so, who negotiates this role with them?

Who prepares them for the role and supports them in it?

Are parents offered training or mentoring in specific skills?

Who negotiates this with them?

Are parents given an on-going record of the child's progress?

Administration

Is there help in linking with other statutory/voluntary/independent services, e.g. for arranging meetings or progress-chasing?

Is there help in record keeping?

Waiting

Do families have to wait after the end of the learning phase for support to begin?

What causes this waiting time?

Can some support be provided during this waiting time?

Integration

To what extent can *all* practitioners who support the child and family integrate their work so that -

* each practitioner knows who else is involved and what their involvement is
* it can be established whether there is any unmet need or duplication of input
* appointments, clinics, home visits, etc. can be rationalised as far as possible
* the daily and weekly timetables of education and therapy are in the best interests of the child and the family
* services provide collectively for the whole child and family

Performance

What is the period of time after referral before the support phase begins?

The Review Phase

A period of support to the child and family must be followed by a reflective process to review progress towards the agreed goals, to consider any changes in abilities and needs, to accommodate any imposed changes in service provision and to agree the next phase or support, i.e. the next family support plan. The sequence now continues with periods of support being followed by review/ planning meetings and new family support plans. This will continue for the pre-school child up to the point where the child and family leave that particular service. At that point the review meeting must plan for continuing support for the child and family over the transition period.

Process

Who co-ordinates the review process for each individual child?
Is there a review meeting?
Who attends it?
What happens to the report of the review process?
Is a new support plan written?

Flexibility

Can the frequency of review meetings vary according to the needs of the child and family?
Can a review be organised at short notice in response to a new situation?

Parents

Can a review meeting be held at the family home if they wish?
Who supports parents during the review phase?
What record are parents given of the review phase?

Administration

Can the administration department organise the review phase in accordance with agreed time periods?
Can there be help with arranging meetings, typing and distributing notes?

Performance

What is the period of time after referral before the review phase begins?

A flexible approach to assessment

Different approaches to the learning phase

Many families of babies and pre-school children who have an identified or suspected long-term condition, disability or special need will be referred in the early stages to the locality's child development team for assessment and support. There might already have been some investigations into the child's condition, abilities and needs. Each child development team or centre will have its own referral criteria which might or might not be formally documented. Some sort of filtering mechanism will already have taken place to bring the child to this part of the pathway. The author is aware of a range of approaches to the learning phase which can be ranged on a spectrum between 'a formal child-assessment event' at one end and 'a family-centred assessment process' at the other.

At the 'formal' end of the spectrum assessments will be designed by practitioners with an emphasis on their own, or their service's, questions and will probably focus primarily on the baby or child. Formal assessments are often delivered as a brief event over one or more days during which the child and family encounter practitioners they have not met before. Each practitioner might ask the parents to retell their story. After what can be a very stressful time parents might be further frustrated to see an untypical snapshot of their child being taken as representative. It can happen that a formal assessments identifies needs but does not result in relevant intervention for the child or family.

At the family-centred end of the spectrum the assessment process is a more drawn-out process in which the child is observed on several occasions in a familiar setting where he or she and parents are relaxed and supported by practitioners they know and trust. Parents are involved in framing questions to be addressed and the assessment process is designed with them to explore approaches to the immediate challenges they are facing at that time as well as to more long-term and general issues.

Observing parents

There is often a third part of the learning phase, typically at the formal end of the spectrum, in which some judgement is made about parents' acceptance of the child's needs, their attitudes to the child and their competence in managing him or her. The results will probably be discussed between practitioners but not discussed with the parents or mentioned in any reports the parents will see.

Two strands within the learning phase

Whether the learning phase focuses on a formal assessment event or a family-centred process there might be two different investigations taking place at the same time. One is the medical investigation of the child to learn as much as possible about the condition, to give it a name if possible and to begin any relevant treatment. The other is the assessment of need in which observation of the child's functioning leads to decisions about relevant interventions from therapists, specialist teachers, Portage teachers, etc.

For most babies and young children with complex needs both the assessment of need and the medical investigation are necessary and they are interdependent; the medical investigation needs information about functioning and the assessment of needs requires information about the medical condition. In fact, the two investigations are often imperceptibly woven together into the assessment.

During the discussions to describe and enhance the integrated pathway there are good reasons for looking at the learning phase in terms of these two different investigations:

1. The resulting pathway diagram will be clearer and more accurate.
2. The discussion should help identify where blockages are happening and why they are happening.
3. The discussion might decide it is possible to continue one of the investigations if the other is delayed for some reason.
4. Parents can be clearer about what outcome to expect from parts of the learning phase, i.e. information about the condition, information about the child's abilities and needs or both.
5. In the same way practitioners can be clearer about what they are offering the child and family at different parts of the learning phase.
6. Practitioners can consider the appropriateness of keeping the strands separate or joining them together at various stages of the pathway, for example, whether to give a meeting with parents a dual function or a single function.

The following chart is an attempt to show the two strands within a generalised assessment procedure and the links between them. Each service will need to make its own version of this diagram to reflect their decisions about how best to link the two investigations in their pathway.

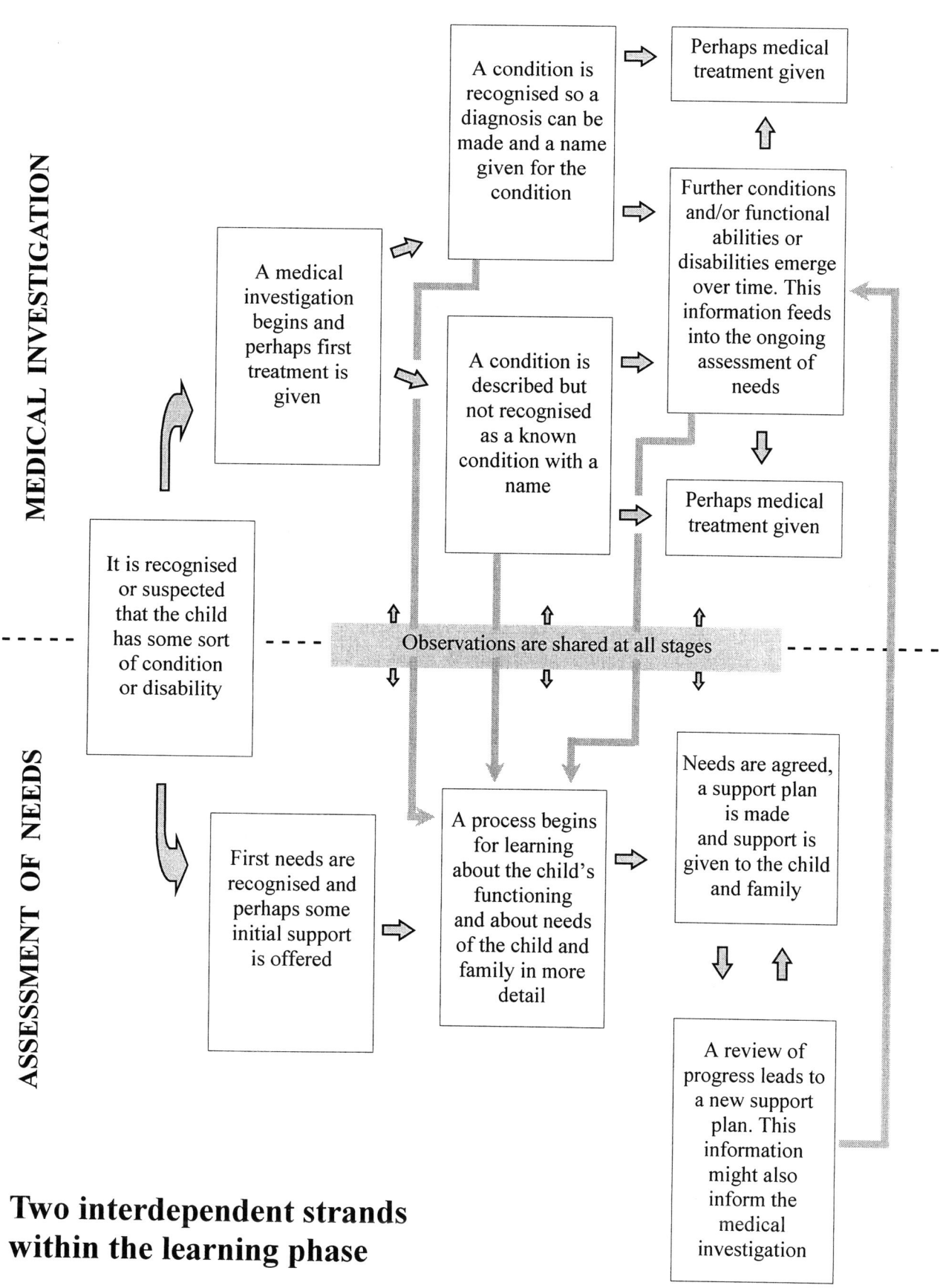

MEDICAL INVESTIGATION

ASSESSMENT OF NEEDS

A condition is recognised so a diagnosis can be made and a name given for the condition

Perhaps medical treatment given

A medical investigation begins and perhaps first treatment is given

Further conditions and/or functional abilities or disabilities emerge over time. This information feeds into the ongoing assessment of needs

A condition is described but not recognised as a known condition with a name

Perhaps medical treatment given

It is recognised or suspected that the child has some sort of condition or disability

Observations are shared at all stages

Needs are agreed, a support plan is made and support is given to the child and family

First needs are recognised and perhaps some initial support is offered

A process begins for learning about the child's functioning and about needs of the child and family in more detail

A review of progress leads to a new support plan. This information might also inform the medical investigation

Two interdependent strands within the learning phase

An Integrated Pathway for Assessment and Support

Agreeing standards for the learning phase

For present purposes an effective assessment procedure can be defined as -

a flexible process which is respectful to the child and family, which gives primacy to the needs expressed by the parents and which considers the abilities and needs of the whole child and the family. It requires practitioners to develop a helping relationship with the child and family. The process includes -

* *answering parents' questions as fully as possible*
* *learning about the child's condition, abilities and needs and about the family situation*
* *listening to the parents' views about the needs of the child and family in order to agree with them a plan for intervention*
* *addressing any immediate stressful situations the family is currently facing*

By this definition the assessment is *not* effective if -

* it is not grounded in helping relationships in which the family and the practitioners know and trust each other
* it does not result in relevant intervention

Standards to aspire to include:

1. The process will be a collaborative effort between parents, practitioners, services and agencies.
2. Duplication of any part of the process by agencies, services or practitioners will be avoided, though there will be a need to follow up some initial investigations with more detailed ones later.
3. The process will be grounded in helping relationships in which the family and key practitioners have time to get to know, trust and feel relaxed with each other.
4. At all stages the parents will be informed, listened to, involved and empowered.
5. Investigations will address questions which have been agreed in advance by parents and practitioners.
6. The two processes of assessment and support will start at the time the child is accepted into the service.
7. The process will be needs-led rather than service-led.

8. The parents will be involved in designing the process for their family.
9. The process will attempt to answer parents' immediate questions and to support them in any particular immediate challenges they are facing. For instance there might be problems in such areas as sleeping, behaviour and feeding which are having a significant impact on the family's wellbeing.
10. Practitioners will not secretly observe parents and will not make collective judgements behind their backs about their competence.
11. The process will result in an agreed written plan of interventions with a date for review.
12. The assessment procedure, whether formal or family-centred, will be accountable with documentation, resources, monitoring and evaluation.
13. Families will not have to languish on a waiting list after referral before assessment begins, nor afterwards for some effective support - even if the full support plan cannot yet be put in place.

How to work towards the last point in this list of standards is the subject of the following section.

Working to reduce waiting times

The ideal is that families will not have to wait for support once they have been accepted into the service. The reasons include:

1. Early intervention and waiting lists are not compatible.
2. For many conditions early diagnosis and intervention improve the prognosis.
3. During the first months and years after becoming aware of the problem, parents are likely to be very vulnerable, confused, anxious and in need of emotional support.
4. The family might be experiencing great stress because of the child's health, behaviour, sleep patterns or nutrition.

Waiting times are often associated with procedures at the 'formal child-assessment event' end of the spectrum. These assessments, which often combine a medical investigation with an assessment of needs, require a large number of people to be in the same place at the same time. Usually they happen within a fixed schedule which caters for a fixed number of children per week or per month. Families have to wait their turn for this expensive resource. This manual offers a model for a more flexible approach to assessment of children with complex needs which is based on observed good practice and which provides some support after referral with minimal waiting times for the child and family.

In this model the service will have two levels of assessment process available to families in its integrated pathway, called here **Level I** and **Level II**. Both will conform as far as possible to the above standards. Both can be fully integrated as necessary with medical investigations.

Level I assessment process

This is carried out by a small number of practitioners who are assigned to the child during the intake process. They might be new to the child or they might already be supporting the family. They are the available key practitioners who can address the needs as they are known at the intake phase.

Each practitioner's brief is to organise one or two sessions with the child and family with the tripartite aim of getting to know them, beginning the assessment/support process and collecting information about the child and family's needs for a planning meeting. The date for the planning meeting might have been decided at the intake phase. The aim of the planning meeting will then be to -

* share observations
* agree needs of the child and family
* agree a first family support plan

The Level I procedure can be co-ordinated by one of the practitioners involved with the family or by another designated during the intake process. If a medical investigation is taking place at the same time there can be links between all the practitioners involved and the two investigations can be integrated at the planning meeting. If the medical investigation is scheduled to be completed after the Level I planning meeting then the integration of both investigations can happen later.

Parents must be involved in the planning process. They will already have exchanged information with each practitioner about the child and the family, about any immediate challenges and about what they are looking for in their support plan. They can be invited to the planning meeting or to a meeting following the planning meeting. In the latter case, they should be given a provisional support plan before the meeting. The purpose of the meeting then is to agree a final version.

The purpose of the Level I assessment process is to get help to the family soon after referral. Support for the child and family does not have to wait for the results of a formal assessment event.

Level II assessment process

In its purpose, this process might equate to the formal child-assessment event in as far as it brings a wider group of practitioners into the process. These practitioners might represent additional disciplines or might bring increased expertise and experience. They represent a larger group than those who will actually support the child and family on a regular basis.

Because it is larger group it might be necessary to carry out part of the process as an event at an agreed time in an agreed place but every effort should be made to be family-centred. Any practitioners whom the family already know and trust should be involved and one particular practitioner should work with the family before the event to reassure, provide information, learn about the child and family, gather their questions and understand any challenges they are facing at the time. This same person should support the family during the assessment.

The practitioners who have met the child and family at or before the event will need now to hold a meeting to share observations, agree needs and create a support plan. Each will already have listened to the parents' view of what the child and family needs and they will bring this information to the meeting. This is likely to be a sizeable conference and it might not be appropriate to invite parents to it. This would be especially stressful for parents if the process has combined a medical investigation with an investigation of needs. However, some services will want to involve parents and some parents would not want to be excluded. If parents are not included, then a small number of key practitioners can meet them at a later time or at a later date to discuss a provisional plan and to finalise the family support plan. In this instance, the service will have to decide whether to use this meeting to discuss two investigations (medical investigation and assessment of needs) at the same time or to hold two separate meetings.

The intake process can determine which practitioners to involve in the Level II procedure, unless it is a team of fixed composition for every child. It can also agree the date or dates for the assessment and can agree the date for giving the family the family support plan.

How Level I and Level II assessments fit into the pathway

The possibilities include:

1. The service might already have an assessment procedure which equates to Level II and this might be felt essential for every child who is accepted into the service. If this leaves some families on a waiting list, they could be offered the Level I procedure as an interim measure to get a first family support plan in place soon after referral.
2. The service has a procedure which equates to Level II but feels that Level I could be more appropriate for some families as they present at referral. This would take some of the pressure off the waiting list for the Level II procedure. The intake process would decide for each family which Level was most appropriate. Families who have the Level I process can later be offered Level II if the need arises.
3. The service already has a procedure which equates to Level I for all the children entering the service and can organise a Level II procedure for particular children as the need arises.
4. The service already has a procedure which equates to Level I and feels this is appropriate for all children entering the service.

In pursuit of early intervention and continuous support the intake panel, or the practitioners designated by the panel to work with the family, can address the following questions in addition to other plans for the family:

1. Is the child and or family already receiving some relevant support? Can it continue beyond the transition into this service? Does anything need to be done to secure the continuation?
2. For some families, can some relevant support for the child and/or family be offered immediately? This might be a series of home visits and/or an offer of a place in a group for the child. This can be thought of as 'first-aid' or a 'holding operation' and might be a very significant contribution to the family's wellbeing.

The next chapter proposes an integrated pathway based on the Team-around-the-Child (TAC) model of multi-agency co-ordination. In this model each family has an individualised team of key practitioners which includes parents. This TAC carries out the Level I assessment process and can create the first family support plan.

Designing an integrated pathway based on the Team-around-the-Child model

The-Team-around-the-Child model

The Team-around-the-Child (TAC) model brings together parents and practitioners, regardless of agency boundaries, into a small individualised team for each particular child with complex needs. It can be defined as an evolving team of those few practitioners who see the child and family on a regular basis to provide practical support in education, therapy and treatment. Parents have a full place in the TAC where their needs are recognised and their central role and expertise are acknowledged. The function of the TAC includes -

* agreeing the needs of the child and family
* agreeing the family support plan
* supporting the child with education, therapy and treatment and supporting other family members as appropriate
* arranging as necessary additional referrals, tests and investigations
* reviewing the support given to the child and family
* reporting as required to other review meetings, case conferences, etc.

Each TAC is led by a Team Leader. This role, which might also be called Keyworker, Co-ordinator, Care Manager, Support Worker, Link Worker, etc. includes -

* chairing the family-friendly TAC meetings
* distributing notes after each meeting
* doing required follow-up
* generally supporting the family through the process

The TAC model has evolved over recent years in response to the widely perceived need for joined-up services and has been shaped by the need to provide a more integrated approach within existing resources. Because service managers adopting this model have usually not been able to recruit new practitioners, the role of Team Leader has been taken on by practitioners already offering support to the child and family. In this 'shared-role' capacity, the role of Team Leader must be clearly defined and delimited as above so that the practitioner can complete the tasks within the time he or she has been allocated. Recognition of the additional role by the practitioner's line manager and administrative support are both essential.

The TAC model satisfies to an extent families' need for a keyworker and gives that person a supportive team and a co-ordinated context in which to operate. For the family the Team Leader is the interface between them and all local services. The Team around the Child represents a scaling down of the large number of helping practitioners to a size the family can relate to and work with. In this model there will be less need for those large case conferences which are so intimidating for some parents.

Practitioners who offer some help to the family but who are not in such close and regular contact are kept in touch with the workings of the TAC by means of the meeting notes and in a continuing two-way communication as necessary. The membership of the TAC will inevitably change as the needs of the child and family change but, by making these changes gradually and with forethought, the TAC as a whole remains a constant source of support.

The TAC operates as a supportive *team* rather than as just a group of practitioners and parents. In this way there is direct benefit to parents who have new opportunities to discuss their child and family with key practitioners all in one place, and to practitioners who might otherwise feel they are isolated and unsupported in their work with the child and family.

The ideal TAC -

> * is encouraging, positive and supportive to all members
> * gives all members an equal voice
> * arrives at collective agreements
> * acknowledges differences of view and negotiates workable solutions

Who can be members of a TAC?

By definition, any practitioner who has close and regular involvement with the child and family should be invited into the TAC. In most cases there will be only a handful of practitioners. Being a member of a TAC does require that practitioner wants to work alongside others with shared commitment and trust. For some TACs this will develop over time and for some practitioners the method of working will be a professional development process. The model does present practitioners with opportunities to develop and extend their abilities in collaborative working and to share some of their skills with practitioners from other disciplines. This development of multi-disciplinary practitioners' ability to view children more holistically and to develop a greater appreciation of the concerns and work of others will be of great benefit in the long-term to this population of children with complex needs in the UK.

Some practitioners have a higher level of training than others and some have greater experience with children with complex needs than others. This difference in expertise will be a factor in the operation of a TAC. It is worth remembering that these differences already occur amongst the practitioners who help children in existing, often fragmented, systems. An effective Team-around-the-Child approach offers a supportive framework for recently trained practitioners and for those new in the field of complex needs. Skilful leadership will acknowledge the greater expertise of some TAC members and draw out fresh perspectives and new approaches of those coming new into this work.

To be a successful approach for all families who need it, the Team-around-the-Child model must be built into a proper system for the locality which is documented, resourced, monitored and evaluated.

This system will offer support to Team Leaders. One approach is the appointment of a Team-around-the-Child Co-ordinator whose role includes -

> * arranging induction, further training and support for Team Leaders

* securing essential resources for Team Leaders
* supporting individual Team Leaders when difficult situations arise
* receiving summarised reports from Team Leaders about work with individual families

A second approach is to nominate a senior practitioner or service manager at the intake process who will be available to the family's Team Leader in a mentoring or supporting capacity. As a routine, this practitioner will receive a copy of the TAC meeting notes.

Essential resources

Team Leaders need time to do the job properly and clerical support. Time is needed for organising meetings, getting notes typed up and distributed and doing any follow-up tasks after each meeting. There are ways of reducing the time commitment, for example, agreeing the date and time of the next TAC meeting at the end of each meeting, using a tape recorder to record notes during the meeting and having clerical help for typing the notes and sending them out. These facilities are valid requirements in a modernising process. But, for a shared-role Team Leader these tasks are additional to the main professional role. Logic dictates that when a busy practitioner agrees to take on some new task, he or she must be relieved of some existing tasks. This does need to be fully acknowledged by line managers and senior managers.

An outline TAC pathway

The following diagram illustrates the journey the child and family make through the service. It shows the 5 phases described on page 7 of Meeting, Learning, Planning, Support and Review. The pathway begins with a single point of entry and is followed by an intake process. A flexible approach is proposed in which the family can be offered a Level II assessment or a 'TAC assessment' which corresponds to Level I.

Outline of an integrated TAC pathway

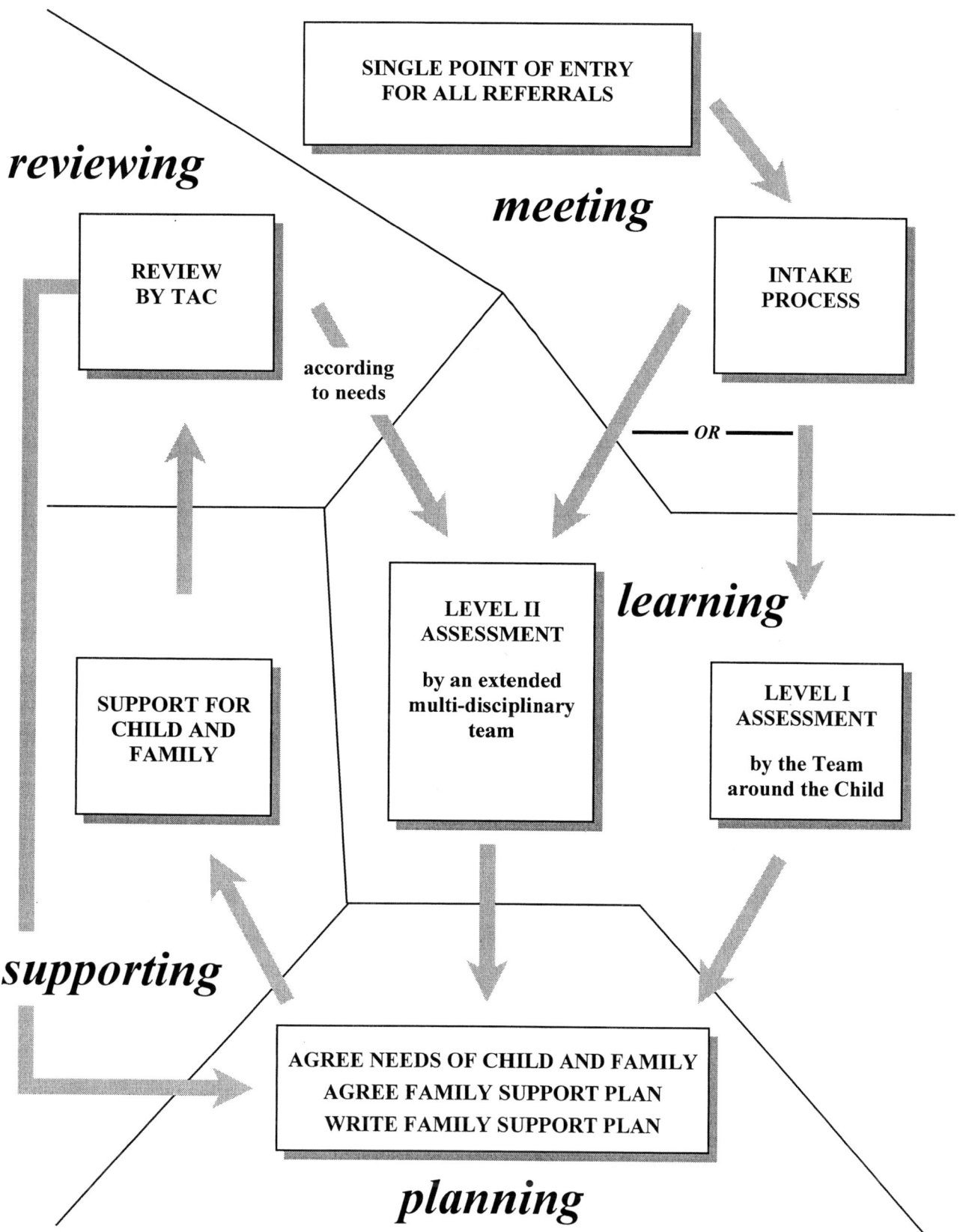

An Integrated Pathway for Assessment and Support

The Meeting Phase

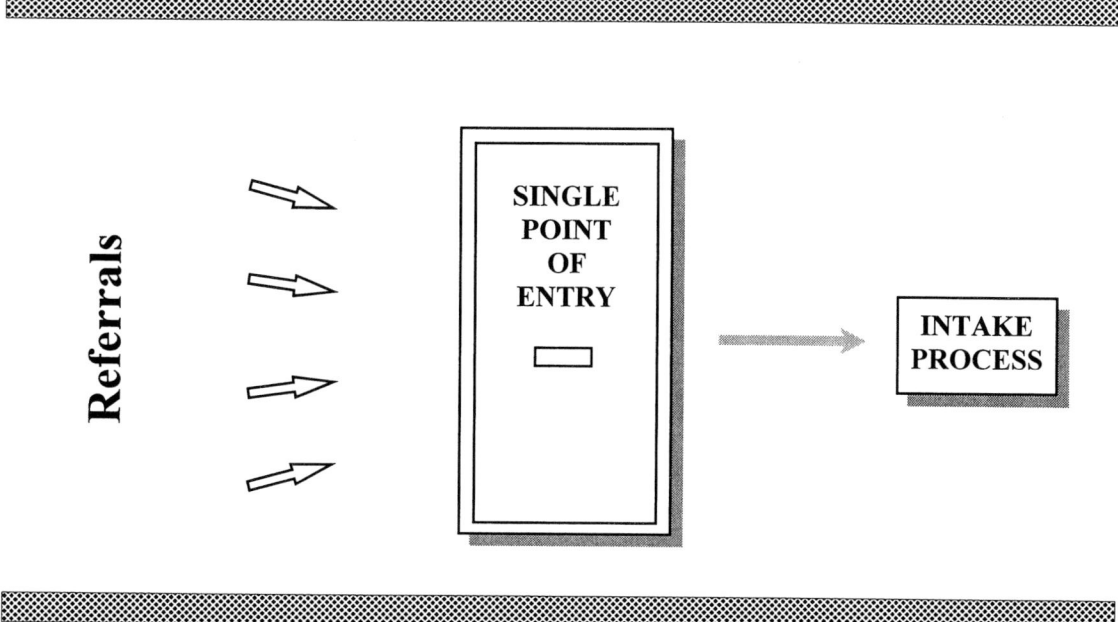

A single point of entry

A pathway into an integrated service requires a single point of entry. If there are several entrances then there are several pathways. The doorway is likely to be an in-tray on the desk of a particular administrator or practitioner. There will need to be clear information disseminated to all people in the service about who this is.

A single point of entry has two major prerequisites. The first is that all potential referring practitioners know where the doorway is and the second is that they know the criteria for referral. To achieve both of these the integrated service needs to publish clear, up-to-date information for distribution to everyone who might refer children. This must include referral criteria and this presupposes an agreement within the integrated service and its managing bodies about which children it can help. This agreement will need to dovetail with other services and agencies in the locality in order that all children are catered for. This is an outcome of a mapping process. Referral criteria will include age, home address and nature of disability.

The service must come to an agreement about whether families can refer themselves. Many parents speak of knowing their child had some sort of condition or disability for months or years before professional acknowledgement. These parents experience great frustration and anger about wasted time and lost opportunities. They speak of having been unable to get beyond their GP or health visitor who did not recognise a problem or wanted to 'wait and see'. These parents assume that specialists would have recognised the condition if they had seen the child. There are very strong arguments in favour of self-referral. One is that it should be part of any service which aims to be responsive to the needs of parents. Another is that specialist practitioners must do all they can to be easily available to concerned parents in the interests of early intervention.

If self-referral is allowed then the service must advertise the fact to parents and practitioners in GP surgeries, clinics, libraries, Citizen Advice Bureaux, etc. (A second approach to this problem is for specialist services to support GPs and health visitors in increasing their awareness about disabilities and special needs.) Parents who do self-refer should be met by a practitioner, perhaps a specialist health visitor or nurse, before their referral is passed to the intake panel.

There should be no filtering at this stage of the pathway. A file is created for each referral making sure there is a name and address for the child, contact details of any referring practitioner and some information about the child. Files are collected and held ready for the next part of the pathway, the intake process.

The intake process

Depending on the structure of the particular service, the initial processing of new referrals will be the responsibility of a multi-disciplinary panel or, where there is wider integration, a multi-agency panel. In the former case the panel will have senior representatives of each discipline and any service co-ordinator or manager. In the latter case the panel will comprise a senior manager from each agency, representatives from each discipline and any service co-ordinator or manager. Some people on the panel will fit more than one of these categories so the panel should not be too large. Seniority is required on this panel because its function is to allocate resources to individual children and families.

This panel should meet regularly enough to minimise the number of referrals to consider at each meeting and to keep each new family's waiting time as short as possible. The task of the panel in relation to each referral includes -

* judging if there is enough information in the file to act on
* confirming that the child and family meet the established criteria
* deciding to accept the child and family into the service
* planning the learning phase and allocating named practitioners to it
* entering the child's information into any multi-agency database

In the longer term the panel can collate information about referrals to keep the relevant directorates informed about changing trends in referral patterns and about consequent changes in required resources.

Discussion by the intake panel, once it has decided it has enough information to accept a child and family into the service, can address the following questions:

1. **Is the child and family already receiving some relevant support?** If they are, can that support continue after they enter this service? For how long? On what conditions does this depend? Are the parents aware of these conditions? These are important questions because parents look for continuity of support and the child will lose opportunities for learning when his or her support is interrupted. If existing support really has to be withdrawn for some inescapable reason, then an overlap should be negotiated so that overall support is continuous even though the particular intervention, or the practitioner or service providing it, has changed.

2. **Can the family be offered some new support immediately?** It may well be that some parts of the service cannot be available at this stage, either because of waiting lists or because more needs to be known about the child. However parents will be reassured to have some support right away. Perhaps there is a practitioner who could make some visits to the home to talk with the parents and perhaps work with the child. Perhaps the child can be invited into a group. Some families at this time will be facing very challenging situations and some support should be offered to them on a 'first-aid' basis.

The initial home visit

Parents might already have waited a long time to get to this stage, they might be upset and anxious, they might be angry about delays, they might have no support systems yet and they might know little or nothing about the service which is now considering offering them support. There are various options for informing and involving parents in the early part of the pathway:

1. Writing to the family to tell them the referral has been received and will be discussed at the next intake panel meeting. The letter can include information about the service, the date and purpose of the meeting and names of people who will be at the meeting.
2. Writing to the parents after the intake panel meeting to welcome them and their child to the service and explain what will happen next.
3. Arranging a home visit before the intake panel meeting. This might be undertaken by a practitioner who knows the family or someone who is new to the family such as a specialist health visitor or nurse.
4. Arranging a home visit after the intake panel meeting. This might be undertaken by the Team Leader if a Team around the Child has been designated.

If no visit is made before the meeting of the intake panel, parents will certainly need some communication after the meeting to tell them their child has been accepted into the service and to invite them to participate in the next part of the pathway. They will need clear information about the service and they will have many questions at this stage. The day and time of this first home visit will be by agreement between the practitioner and parents. Depending on the practitioner's working pattern this might need to be early evening to accommodate a working parent. Such a meeting will have many functions   and proper time should be allocated to it (between 1 and 2 hours). This initial meeting provides an opportunity to -

* start building a trusting relationship with the family
* begin the assessment/support process
* be positive about the child and about the parents' caring
* be reassuring about the service and what it will entail
* answer, as far as possible, very many questions
* learn about what has happened to the family
* find out what particular challenges they are facing at the moment
* start learning about needs in general

Parents will have a story to tell and will probably welcome talking to a practitioner who can empathise and who has good listening skills. Parents might not have been afforded this essential facility before. Listening at this level is itself a therapeutic intervention.

This family story will include the child's history, medical and otherwise, and this should be recorded in detail so that it can be typed up afterwards. This record can then be passed to other members of the TAC and other practitioners by agreement so that they do not have to ask those first questions again. This sharing of information will be within the rules of confidentiality that the family have already agreed to.

It is very important that the typed record is given back to the parents before distribution so that they can agree it or modify it. This is probably the first written version of the family story and will become part of a lasting record. It is crucial that the parents are comfortable with it.

After deciding to accept the child into the service and addressing the above questions, the intake panel will consider how best to organise learning about the child and family. This is discussed in the next section.

The Learning Phase

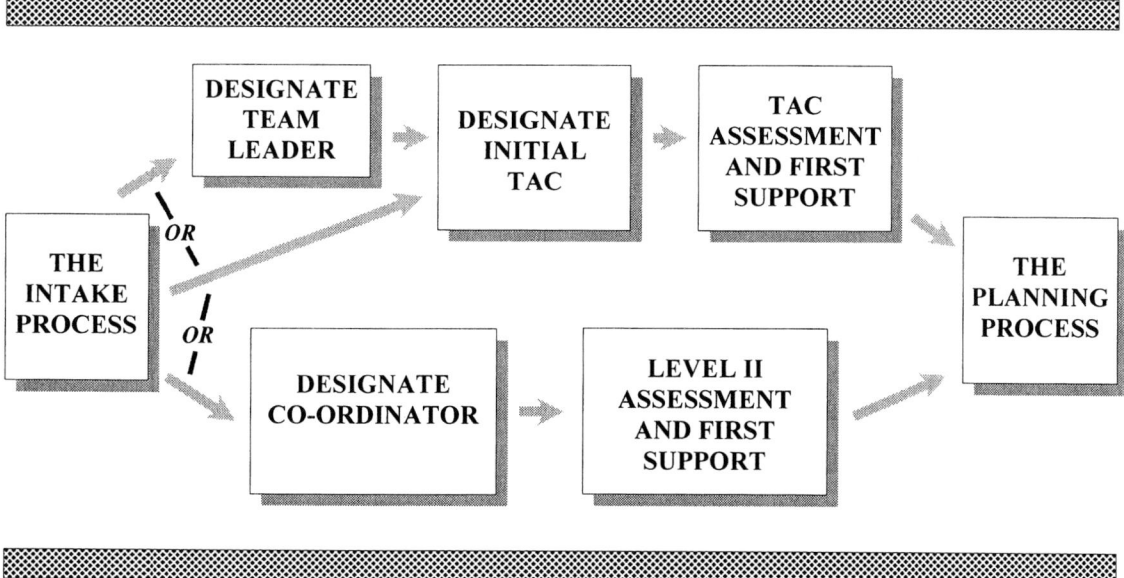

The major role of the intake panel, after agreeing that the child and family meet the service's entrance criteria, is to plan how best to learn more about the child and family so that a first family support plan can be agreed. There are two options:

1. The panel will feel that the Team-around-the-Child assessment process is adequate and appropriate at this stage. The panel can then designate the members of the TAC or they can designate just the Team Leader. The panel can agree about any medical investigation that will take place at the same time and with which the TAC assessment can be integrated.

2. The panel will feel that a Level II assessment is the most appropriate way to proceed. The panel can arrange some 'first-aid' support if the family is facing particular challenges and they can discuss how other relevant support can be offered to the child and family during any waiting period before the assessment begins.

The TAC assessment process

To take this option means that the members of the intake panel feel enough is known about the child and family to be able to identify which key practitioners need to be closely involved at this time. This might comprise as few as two or three. These practitioners, defined by their present or potential regular and practical involvement, form the first Team around the Child. The intake panel will designate a practitioner to be the Team Leader for the TAC. The panel can also set a date for completion of the written family support plan.

The discussion about who should be Team Leader must acknowledge the views of parents but it might not be possible to offer them a free choice. Perhaps in the locality's system not all practitioners can take on this added task. Whether or not the particular practitioner is the choice of the parent, Team Leaders should have the necessary skills and attitudes to be able to form an honest, trusting and respectful relationship with parents within one or two visits. This is certainly within the scope of the majority of practitioners but there will inevitably be occasions when parent and practitioner cannot relate to each other effectively.

There might be an agreed need for one or more practitioners in the TAC who simply are not available, perhaps because no one is in post, because of leave or because of agreed work patterns in the service. The TAC system does not remedy this. It merely requires that the practitioners who are available work together in a cohesive team with parents and regardless of agency boundaries. Informing parents about any lack of required practitioners is a necessary part of an honest partnership. With that information parents can make their own informed approach to responsible bodies if they wish. The intake panel can also keep a record of these shortfalls for strategic planning.

The task of the Team Leader now is to co-ordinate an assessment/support process during which each TAC member organises one or two first sessions with the child and family to offer support, learn more about the child and family and to carry out necessary investigation procedures. These sessions can happen at home or elsewhere by mutual agreement. They can take place in any nursery or group setting where the child is placed. Practitioners can arrange to do these sessions on their own or they can do joint sessions with another TAC member.

It is stating the obvious to say that parents will have their own questions about their child's abilities and needs. A needs-led service will give these questions equal weight in the learning phase or even accord them the highest priority.

There is a clear rationale for this. Practitioners are likely to want to recruit the help of parents in working with the child as co-workers once some goals have been agreed. They will be most motivated to work towards goals which address their concerns.

Also, parents who are struggling to cope and to keep the family in one piece will value goals which are relevant to their struggle more than goals which appear irrelevant or peripheral. Goals which focus on behaviour, sleep, feeding and crying might be the priority for stressed parents. This does not mean other areas of development are ignored. This manual advocates setting integrated or holistic goals for children with complex needs in which movement, posture, perception, communication and cognition components are combined in some way.

Learning about the child at this stage should include conversations with any other practitioners who know, or have known, the child and can include observation of the child in any placement.

This part of the integrated pathway can have variations either in relation to individual needs or in how the service has chosen to design the pathway:

1. It might be thought appropriate for the key practitioners to get together with each other after the intake process before they arrange their sessions with the child and family. This can be a useful meeting especially if the practitioners do not already know each other or are not sure what each other's role with the family is. This would be a valuable occasion for building familiarity and trust.
2. There could be a first meeting of the TAC with parents after the intake process before the practitioners meet the family individually. This would depend on time available and on the views of the parents and practitioners.
3. The intake panel might elect the Team Leader for the child and family and then devolve to him or her the task or creating the first Team around the Child for the initial assessment/support process. The Team Leader can first meet with the family to involve them in deciding who should be in the TAC.

Overseeing the TAC assessment process

The intake panel can assign one of its members or another senior practitioner or manager to work with the Team Leader to oversee the work of the TAC. This provides the Team Leader with support additional to that from his or her line manager. This practitioner can attend the review meetings or receive a copy of the review report.

The Level II assessment

This facility can be made available by the service for children and families as required. It can be triggered by the intake panel or later by the TAC at review stage. In some services it might need to be modelled on the 'formal child-assessment event' described earlier but if so, care should be taken to make the process as family-centred and as unthreatening as possible. Because it brings in a wider group of practitioners, some of whom might be based elsewhere, it might not be as flexible and as adaptable to each particular family's needs as the TAC approach. For this reason it will be necessary for the TAC Team Leader to offer additional support to the family. The Level II assessment will probably have a shared function of assessment of needs and a medical investigation.

In services where the Level II assessment is not automatic for every child, the intake panel can opt for one when they feel they know much less about a particular child's condition, abilities and needs than they know about most children at this stage and feel that the TAC is unlikely to find all the answers on its own.

The Level II assessment can be co-ordinated by a senior practitioner, a service manager or the TAC Team Leader and will follow an agreed and accountable procedure which is documented, resourced, monitored and evaluated.

In the event of a Level II assessment being triggered at the intake process, the child and family should be offered some relevant support as well. This will depend on what is known about the child and family and whether or not it is appropriate at that stage to create a TAC. Whatever the situation, support of some sort should be made available after the intake process.

The Planning Phase

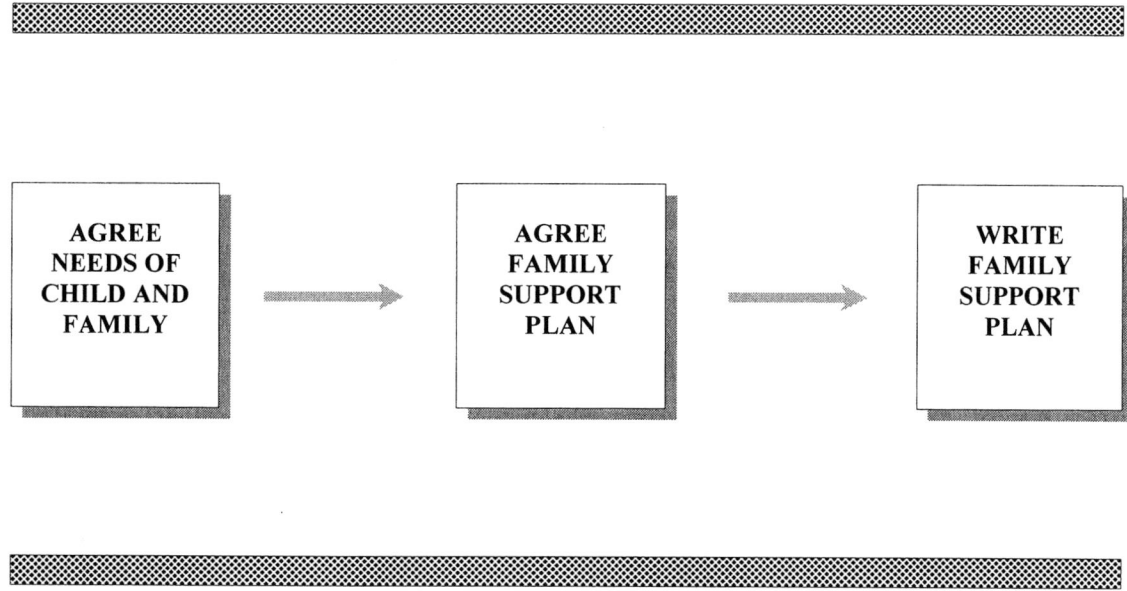

The planning phase after a TAC assessment process

In the case of a TAC assessment, after an agreed period of time devoted to the initial assessment/support process, practitioners and parents come together in a first Team-around-the-Child meeting. Their discussion is guided by the Team Leader to include the following:

1. Sharing general observations about the child's condition, abilities and needs and about the family's situation.
2. Agreeing a list of the child and family's needs. This will probably comprise -

   * needs which can be met by the present TAC members
   * needs which require involvement of, or referral to, other practitioners (who might become TAC members if they will have a regular involvement)

* needs which involve other agencies, (e.g. housing, counselling)
* needs for which local agencies have no remedy at present

3. Agreeing the content of the written family support plan. This should include agreed goals.
4. Agreeing the date, time and venue for the next TAC meeting to review progress.

This discussion should address the situation of the child and family as it is now and anticipate changes during the period up to the next TAC meeting. There will be an emphasis on listening to parents' views with some focus on the particular challenges the family are facing at the moment. There will need to be agreement about any role parents will have as co-workers in the work with the child and decisions about the support they will be offered to help them succeed in this role. There should be decisions about any need to involve other practitioners at this stage and about the need for any additional tests and investigations. Practitioners can agree who will chase up any appointments for clinics, tests, etc. which should have happened by now but have not. Such follow-up does not have to be the task of the Team Leader if one of the other TAC members is more appropriate.

The initial family support plan will include -

* a list of TAC members with description of their role and contact details
* a list of other involved practitioners with role and contact details
* Team Leader's contact details with times when he or she can be contacted and the timescale for replying to messages
* what contact the family can expect from the TAC if the child is admitted to hospital and how the normal service will resume after discharge
* how often and where the TAC members will see the child and family
* the goals set by TAC members
* referrals to be made to other practitioners and agencies and who will make them
* the involvement of parents in working towards agreed goals
* any integration of interventions, e.g. joint sessions
* the agreed rules for confidentiality within the service
* procedures for making a complaint

(General information covering the last two points might already have been given to the family in a letter or brochure about the service.)

To complete this process, the Team Leader writes the initial family support plan for distribution to an agreed list of people which will include the parents, TAC members and other practitioners in the wider group. A medical investigation might be happening at the same time. If so, there will be necessary links between the two processes.

If the Team Leader has access to clerical support with audio-typing, then the notes from the TAC meeting can be dictated during the meeting. This has the dual advantage of agreeing the notes with all members and saving the Team Leader's time after the meeting.

In this integrated model, the family support plan is an official multi-disciplinary or multi-agency document which records a joint assessment of needs combined with an agreed action plan. This assessment is a process rather than an event and is a supportive interaction with the child and family rather than just the completion of an assessment form. It might be, however, that two or more local agencies have already worked together to create a combined assessment form. This can be completed at this stage but it will not replace the written family support plan.

The planning phase after a Level II assessment procedure

The Level II assessment will gather a body of information which must now be fed into the planning process.

The practitioners who carried out the assessment can meet to share observations, to discuss the child's condition, abilities and needs and the family's situation and to plan how to support the child and family. This assessment has probably investigated both the medical condition and the needs of the child and family and so there might be a large number of people at the meeting. If parents are attending they will need careful support before, during and after the meeting. Some services do not invite parents to such meetings and some parents will decline if invited. If a TAC is already in place its members will be involved in this meeting. The Team around the Child as a whole or the Team Leader can take the proposed plan to the family later if the parents did not attend.

If the TAC is not in place at this stage the practitioners at this meeting can consider who should be in the TAC or they can pass their assessment report and recommendations back to the intake panel. This will depend on where the authority to allocate resources lies. Either way, the end result should be the designation of a Team around the Child and an agreed family support plan.

Agreeing the role of parents as co-workers

It is not appropriate to assume parents will take on a co-working role with practitioners in their work towards agreed goals. Their involvement will need to be properly negotiated with them, perhaps by each practitioner or by the Team Leader. There are many factors influencing the negotiation:

1. Are parents at this early stage emotionally ready, or are they too upset, confused and anxious about the child?
2. Are they getting enough sleep at night to be ready for this task?
3. Do they have too many other big issues on their mind, e.g. relationship problems, money worries, anxiety about the child's health and survival?
4. Do they have enough time during the day (or when they get home from work)?
5. Are siblings competing for their attention?
6. Is there space in the home for the activity and necessary equipment?
7. Does the parent prefer to remain as 'just a parent'?

Most parents will want to help as much as possible with the work at some point if not at this early stage when they are still struggling to adjust and cope. When parents want to be co-workers there are other issues to consider to make their co-working successful for themselves and the child:

1. Does the parent see the relevance of the goal?
2. Does the parent *really* understand the approach (i.e. What he or she has to do)? The approach might need to be demonstrated many times. Written notes and diagrams will help. A video tape will help even more.
3. Can the work be integrated into play activity or into everyday routines, e.g. bath time, dressing, mealtime?
4. Is the activity enjoyable for the child and the parent?
5. Is the parent being given too many co-working tasks?

Integrated goals

The TAC provides an ideal opportunity for practitioners and parents to agree a whole approach to development and learning with integrated goals. For babies and young children, an integrated or holistic goal is one which relates to a play activity or a daily living activity and which is not limited to a single developmental area, e.g. motor, perception, communication, cognition. The integrated goal recognises that children do not function in this discipline-specific way. The integrated goal will appear relevant to the parents and motivating to the child.

There is always the danger of overloading the child and parents with too many suggestions and goals. This is especially true when practitioners work separately from each other in a fragmented approach. The TAC meeting is a good opportunity to anticipate this danger and to prioritise goals. This will allow the child and parents to focus on one or more goals now while leaving others to tackle later. Each integrated goal should not demand too much new learning at one time. It can comprise one or more elements which the child had already mastered fully, one or more elements which the child has learned and still needs to practice and one or more elements which represent new learning.

The Support Phase and The Review Phase

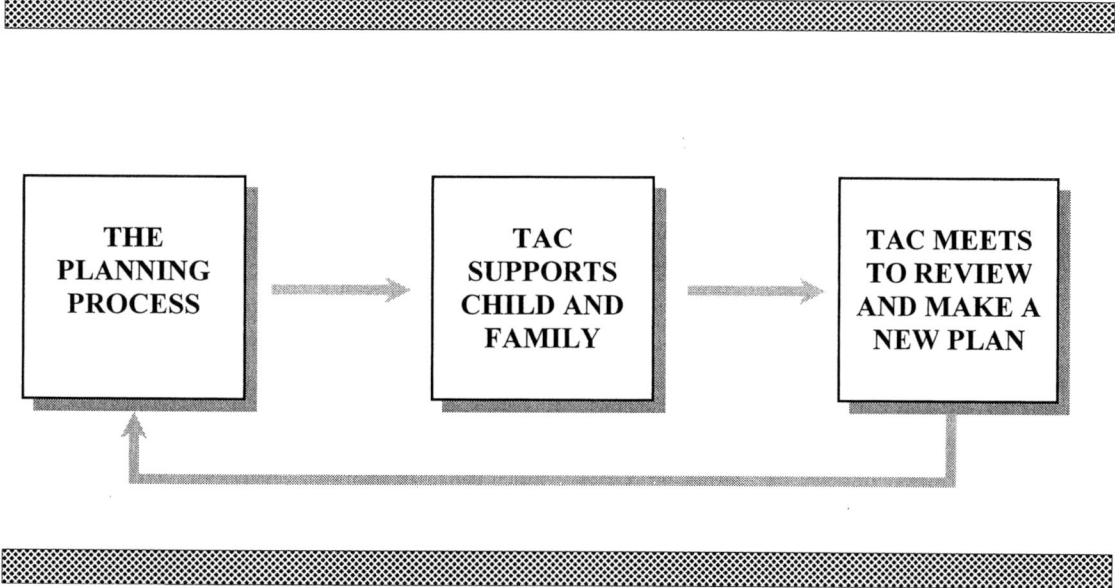

The support phase

There is now a written family support plan which has been agreed by practitioners and parents and which sets a date for the TAC to meet again to review progress and agree a new plan. Each family support plan only lasts for this agreed period between TAC meetings, and that period will depend on several factors including how quickly the situation of the family and the child is changing. The period can be shorter when everything is in a state of flux and then less frequent when things are more settled. In the latter situation meetings might be between three and six times a year. It is likely that with most families the Team Leader's task will be more demanding in the first months after meeting a new family. However, major changes and crises which require increased support can occur at any time.

Practitioners have already been getting to know the family and providing first support and they continue now according to the agreed plan. Practitioners might stay separate in their work or they might agree to join together for particular sessions.

There is an opportunity within the TAC model for practitioners to dissolve professional boundaries to some extent by agreeing that one or two practitioners will predominate in delivering the agreed integrated approach to the child and family. This will represent a reduction in the number of people doing hands-on work with particular children for whom too many pairs of hands can be counter-productive. This arrangement requires that the practitioners know and trust each other well enough to exchange some skills. Taken further, this integration of inputs becomes the primary provider model in which practitioners hand over their programme to one person who then works with the child and family holistically. Professional expertise is not diluted because each practitioner hands over only those parts of the child's programme which are appropriate. Each practitioner maintains contact with the child and family to offer more specialist parts of the programme, to observe the child's progress and to modify the approach. The parts of a programme handed over in this way might equate more or less to the work given to a parent who is co-working. Nursery nurses are already accustomed to working in this way in various settings. There is a role for generic support workers to work with children in this way in their own homes.

The service will need to decide how the work of the TAC is to be recorded. The TAC meeting notes are one part of this process and the family has copies. Each practitioner might keep his or her own record of each session with the child and family. The family can be provided with a family-held record which records all work with the child towards the agreed goals. This might be integrated into the document holding the family support plan. In the One Hundred Hours service families were offered 'A Whole-Picture Book' which listed each agreed goal with plenty of space for comments about progress towards the goal. In the case of integrated goals, the work can be offered to the child by more than one practitioner, by parents and other family members and by workers in any placement the child attends. If the record stays with the child then everyone will know what the goals are and can help in the work towards them. These people can then write their comments. Such a record can be a loose-leaf format so space is not restricted. At each review meeting, pages for achieved goals can be removed to store elsewhere and new pages added.

The review phase

At the end of the allotted period of work the TAC meets to review progress and write a new family support plan. A date is fixed for the next TAC meeting. If the TAC meeting marks a significant change in service provision, perhaps at a transition into a nursery or school, the family support plan must reflect the change and allow for only a gradual change in membership of the TAC. In this way support to the child and family will not be disrupted. At this time also there might be an agreement to change the Team Leader. This would ideally happen after a period of overlap rather than at the same time as other major changes.

The tasks at the first review meeting include:

1. Sharing general observations about the child's condition, abilities and needs and about the family situation.
2. Sharing observations about how well the TAC model is working for the family.
3. Sharing views on how well the recording process is working.
4. Considering any changes in support imposed by service providers.
5. Reviewing the child's progress towards the agreed goals and setting new goals.
6. Reviewing parents' role as co-workers.
7. Reviewing support offered to parents and other family members.
8. Considering whether the TAC should stay as it is, invite new members or lose a present member and agree a gradual approach for the change.
9. Agreeing any additional referrals, tests and investigations.
10. Considering if a Level II assessment is required (if the system allows for this).
11. Writing a new family support plan.
12. Agreeing a date, time and venue for the next TAC meeting.

If a Level II assessment is available, the review meeting can opt for this when -

*   planned interventions have resulted in significantly less progress than predicted
*   TAC members feel they need to discuss the child with practitioners who have different or additional expertise
*   there is some unresolved difference of view between practitioners and parents or between practitioners themselves about the child's condition or the child's or family's needs

There might be a situation in which parents are more often than not at loggerheads with their practitioners about the support offered to themselves and to the child. The approaches to resolve this include:

1. A Level II assessment to attempt to resolve questions about the child's condition, abilities and needs.
2. Some intervention by a senior practitioner or service manager to find a negotiated way forward.

These two approaches can be used together.

In conclusion

Modernisation at the national level

Because this manual is grounded in good practice occurring in many parts of the UK and Ireland and because the ideas within it are the result of detailed discussions with parents, practitioners, service managers and teams within health, education, social services and the voluntary/independent sector, it is hoped that it will be relevant to all services and agencies which are working now to develop integrated pathways for children with complex needs and their families.

The manual is offered also as a contribution to a wider debate about services for these children and their families. The National Service Framework for Children, which is being developed at the time of writing, is probably going to require services to provide an integrated approach for children with complex needs and their families. The NSF consultation documents suggest that families should have joint assessments and that families of children with a high level of need should be offered a keyworker. This will be a welcome message which will empower all people who strive to modernise these services but it will raise many questions. For example, what will a keyworker do? Who can be a keyworker? What form will a joint assessment take? What should an integrated service look like?

This will be a very stimulating and far-reaching debate during the coming years. The National Service Framework consultation document suggests that disabled children should receive high standards of care and support provided by staff who have appropriate training, skills and competencies. How should we define a high standard of care for the families of children with complex needs? What skills should the practitioners for these families have? Should there be special training for working with this group of children? What competencies should a practitioner have for being involved in the assessment of these children?

Many of these questions must be directed at professional associations and societies. To identify effective answers the professional bodies in education, nursing, medicine, therapy, social work, psychology, etc. must find ways to work together on a joined-up approach to setting standards and protocols for work with children with complex needs. If they produce separate responses little will be achieved. This is a great challenge.

Modernisation at the local level

Practitioners, parents, services and agencies who are working to create an integrated pathway in their locality also face a great challenge. This should not be underestimated. Essential requirements in this drive for modernisation include a multi-agency management group, the involvement of parents in the planning process, investment of adequate time for planning and careful management of change.

A multi-agency management group

This comprises senior managers from the separate agencies. There can be little progress towards integration without a joined-up driving force at senior level. Its members will need to be committed to radical change and to the allocation of resources to it. Once this groups is formed it should be positioned within the complex network of strategic committees across the agencies. This process should also indicate where the multi-agency group can tap into available funding streams.

Representative parents

The multi-agency management group should include representative parents. It is not advisable to assume parents will want to attend meetings on their own. There needs to be a mechanism for these parents to be properly representative of other parents in the locality. Ideally, a parents' forum will send representatives to the multi-agency group and will debate the issues which arise. There is nothing to prevent parents being offered a fee for their contribution and help with transport and child care.

Time

Time is essential. The creation of an integrated pathway will take time at all stages of its development and at all levels within agencies. The members of the multi-agency management group, managers and practitioners involved should be allocated sufficient time for the task. This will inevitably impact on services but it is an essential investment without which there will be no real modernisation.

Management of change

The integrated pathway requires practitioners within each agency to change how they work. It also requires agencies and services to change to more collaborative working. These are massive changes to contemplate and many practitioners will feel threatened. Others will feel a sense of relief that their good practice is being recognised at last. The process of changing to more integrated working must inform and involve and inspire practitioners at all levels from the start. No new integrated systems will succeed unless the practitioners want to work together and want to work in genuine partnership with parents. There is much work to be done across services and agencies to support practitioners in learning about each other's work and concerns, to encourage a softening of professional boundaries and to generate trust in each other.

Sources of further information

The Handsel Trust
62 Johnson Road, Erdington, Birmingham, B23 6PY.
Tel/fax: 0121 373 2747. E-mail: handsel@LineOne.net

The Handsel Trust publishes books about family support one of which details
the role and protocols of the keyworker in the One Hundred Hours project:
The Keyworker: a practical guide by Gudrun Limbrick-Spencer.

Social Policy Research Unit
Professor Patricia Sloper, Senior Research Fellow.
University of York, Heslington, York, YO10 5DD.
Tel: 01904 433608. E-mail: SPRU@york.ac.uk

Care Co-ordination Network UK
SPRU, University of York, Heslington, York, YO10 5DD.
Tel: 01904 433608. E-mail: kb17@york.ac.uk

Norah Fry Research Centre
3 Priory Road, Bristol, BS8 1TX.
Tel: 0117 923 8137. Fax: 0117 946 6553. E-mail: R.Townsley@bristol.ac.uk

The Centre for Parent and Child Support
Professor Hilton Davis, Director.
Munro Centre, 66 Snowsfield, London, SE1 3SS.
Tel: 0207 378 3255. Fax: 0207 378 3243. E-mail: linda.fone@kcl.ac.uk

Documents

Together from the Start - *Practical guidance for professionals working with
disabled children (birth to 2) and their families*
Department for Education and Skills and Department of Health.

Special Educational Needs Code of Practice
Department for Education and Skills.

Framework for the Assessment of Children in Need and their Families
Department of Health.

The National Service Framework for Children
Department of Health.